Form Drawing
Grades One through Four

by
Laura Embrey-Stine
Ernst Schuberth

RUDOLF STEINER COLLEGE PRESS

ISBN: 0-945803-35-4

Rudolf Steiner College Press
9200 Fair Oaks Boulevard
Fair Oak, CA 95628

FOREWORD

The need for a book of this kind became apparent during a summer session Waldorf teacher training course at Rudolf Steiner College in Sacramento, California in 1996. Ernst Schuberth, the instructor of that course, then collaborated with one of his students, Laura Embrey-Stine, to write a book that would provide Waldorf teachers with a guide to teaching form drawing in grades one through four. The ideas from the above-mentioned course are presented here, along with a possible sequence of forms. This book is written especially for Waldorf teachers, who already possess a basic understanding of child development according to Anthroposophy and Waldorf pedagogy.

INTRODUCTION

Rudolf Steiner gave indications for the teaching of form drawing during his lecture courses at Stuttgart in 1919. Form drawing is one element that is unique to Waldorf education. Even upon introduction to form drawing, teachers see that form drawing is a powerful tool for development in a child's education. The purpose of this book is to aid teachers in deepening their understanding of form drawing, why it is done and where it leads.

There are many sound reasons which support the feeling that form drawing is good for children. The simplest and perhaps most straight-forward reason is that it develops the fine motor skills as a preparation, and later a support, for writing. It strengthens eye-hand coordination, giving the eye practice at being coachman for the horses, the hands. Form drawing also works in the other direction: The movement of the hand also educates the brain. Furthermore, it is part of the evolution of art and, as such, develops the aesthetic sense and a feeling for form. It also teaches thinking but in a non-intellectual way; it trains the intelligence to be flexible, able to follow and understand a complicated line of thought. The more human beings are trained to think flexibly, the greater the world is strengthened in intelligence. Finally, form drawing really supports the development of the whole being of the child, guiding it in a healthy way with certain types of forms brought to the child which are appropriate for his age in the various grades. The sequence of forms given in this book especially meets this requirement.

The teacher should be aware not only of why he is teaching form drawing in the wider sense, but also he should himself be aware of what effect that particular form will have on the children before he presents it. He can only have this if he develops in himself an inward feeling for form, a feeling for the character of the curvature of the line. In the curvature of the line lies the will impulse; the stronger the curve, the stronger the will impulse.

Developing a feeling for form, then, develops the will forces. To develop this feeling for form, the hands must be brought to feel the form; we need to *see* with our hands. We need to describe the feeling

1. Rudolf Steiner, *Practical Advice for Teachers* (London, U.K.: Rudolf Steiner Press, 1970).

of the movement. We need to work through a form until it is incorporated in us; the drawing itself is really only a trace, an echo, of our *process of movement*. Although we wish to achieve a "certain perfection" in the drawing of the form, it is the process which is of the greater importance. If the process has been properly worked through, the product will be good.

The movement, then, is of great importance. The final product is as well. It should be remembered that the line is the subject and it is *not* a picture of something in the outer world, even if the shape of the form suggests a butterfly or some other object. It is not in keeping with the purposes of form drawing to permit children to draw little flowers, faces, Christmas trees, etc. inside or around the form they have drawn, either. These detract from the line. The teacher may tell a story which describes the movement of the form to bring the movement into connection with the child's soul. (Some examples of these will be given.) Of equal importance to the line and its movement is the space between the lines of the form; this space should not be filled with irrelevancies. It *is* important for the children to connect with the form in the feeling life. Color, used appropriately, can serve this purpose developing the children's aesthetic senses as well. Colors should be chosen that are harmonious and that suit the form; they should be used in such a way that they enhance, not detract from, the beauty and movement of the form.

In developing a feeling for form, a feeling for the curvature of the line, it is also important to develop a feeling for the width of the line. By fourth grade, this matters very much in the work with the knotted forms. The character of the whole form is affected by how the line is narrower here, how it widens there, how it comes to a point here, how it curves softly there. If one draws the line carefully, one has to care whether it is wide or narrow, and one connects oneself to the form through the feelings.

Dear colleagues, please do not take this book as the final word on teaching form drawing in a Waldorf School. No dogmatism is intended here. This is only one way to approach the teaching of form drawing, a subject which intrinsically lends itself to endless creativity. At the end of this book, additional references are listed which may offer further insight and inspiration. Keep form drawing alive for your children and yourself by finding your own way, using this approach as a guide, a place to begin.

If we follow the indications of Rudolf Steiner given in the 1919 teacher training course, we begin in first grade with the straight line and the curved line. In the first year, the child gains uprightness and later, around one year, she learns to walk. In this upright posture the child actually draws the vertical straight line with her body. Now in first grade, she is able to draw the line outside her body and look at it. In order to be able to do this properly she must have developed a feeling of balance in the body, a perception of her own body. She must have developed a coordination of the balance and movement senses, an enormous task of the human Ego working unconsciously in the will forces. The straight line has a connection with the Ego.

The curved line is softer, more connected with the environment. When I look around me, I draw a curved line with my gaze. With the curve, there is a differentiation between what is inside and what is outside. The curve gives the feeling that it could be part of a whole.

In eurythmy, the soul force of thinking draws the straight line and the soul force of willing forms the curved lines. In form drawing, then, exercises with the straight line are more connected with the development of thinking, while exercises with the curved line are more connected with the development of will. The polarity of the human being lies in these two types of lines. These two streams are basically separated at the beginning of grade one. On the first day of first grade both are introduced.

<u>Day One</u>: Saying, "Watch me do this," the teacher goes to the blackboard and very slowly and carefully, almost as slowly as possible, draws a straight vertical line, not too small, from top to bottom (see Figure 1). The children will be engaged in their whole being; having already been told why they come to school, they will have a sense that this activity of the teacher is the first great revelation of many to come in their education. When the line has been drawn, the teacher turns to the children and says, "Now take your hand and do it, too!" Then the children should practice making this line slowly in as many ways as possible. They may stand up and see and feel that their bodies make a straight vertical line. They may draw the line in the air, very slowly, with their fingers, with their noses, with their chins, with their eyes. They may draw it with their feet on the floor. They may walk a line, heel to toe.

Figure 1: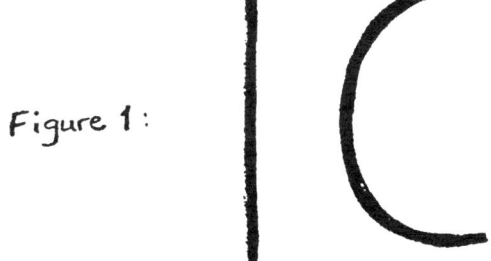

1

It is of great importance that they should have much practice before actually drawing the line, that they should really feel the line within them. They may practice on the blackboard (the teacher should start her line low enough that the children can begin theirs at the same height; they do not like to start lower! or they can use a chair to stand on), then above the paper on their desks. Then the teacher says, "Now I am going to do this," and draws a curved line (see Figure 1), "and now you take your hands and do it, too." When they have practiced as they did with the straight line, the teacher says, "This one is a straight line and this one is a curved line." (It is important that the teacher name the lines. If the teacher gives the name, the teacher has the authority. If the children give the name, they have the authority. The teacher has an opportunity here to develop the children's feeling for authority in the right way.) The teacher can then ask, "What is the feeling of the curved line? Is it different from the feeling of the straight line?" Discussion about these questions begins to develop in the children a feeling for form. At last, they may draw the line. If they have practiced enough, they will achieve a "certain perfection" in their drawing, which, Rudolf Steiner has indicated, is desirable. The drawing itself is only a trace, an outer manifestation of the process of movement, the inner activity of the child. The process is of the greatest importance; herein lies the power of transformation.

Day Two: In the next lesson, the teacher draws the two lines again, asking individual children, "What is this?" The child answers, "A straight line!" Pointing to the curved line, the teacher asks a child, "Now what is this?" The child answers, "A curved line!" (The teacher does *not* say, "What did we do yesterday?" or the children will think, "The teacher should know what we did!" and the teacher's authority will be undermined.) Some discussion and practice of these lines ensues and the children may draw them in their main lesson books.

Figure 2: _____

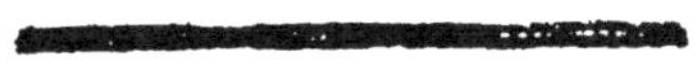

Then the teacher slowly draws, from left to right, a horizontal line (see Figure 2) and tells the children, "This is a straight line lying down." Then the teacher asks, "What is the feeling of this line? How is it different from the first straight line we made?" If the teacher asks how they might make this line with their bodies, they may be brought to feel that this line is resting; the line may then be named "the resting line" This gives the children a picture: "horizontal" is too abstract. After practicing this line as they did the two previous lines, they may draw it in their books.

Day Three: The next exercise with the straight line comes the following day with the combination of the upright, standing line and the horizontal line (see Figure 3). Figure 3a may be described as a human being standing on the Earth. Figure 3b may be the upright human being with arms stretched out to embrace the world. Figure 3c could be described as the human being standing between Earth and sky. The next form in the straight line stream is the slanted, or leaning line (see Figure 4). Discuss the nature of the line with the children (Is it "tired"?); this develops within them the feeling for form, an understanding that form and direction are related. Then they may bring the

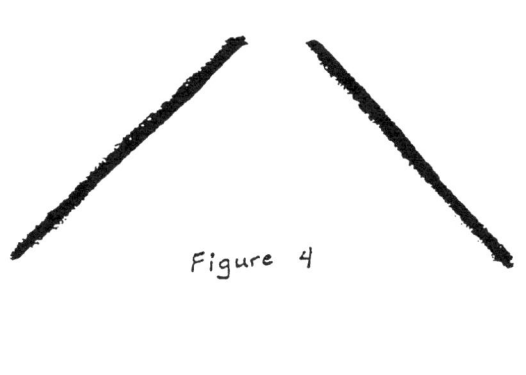

Figure 4

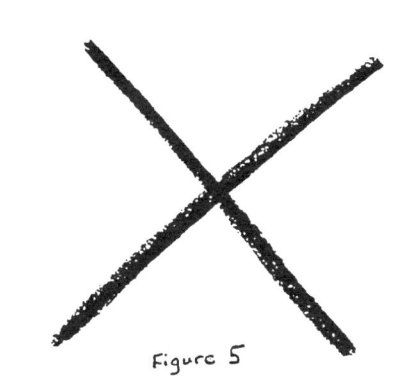

Figure 5

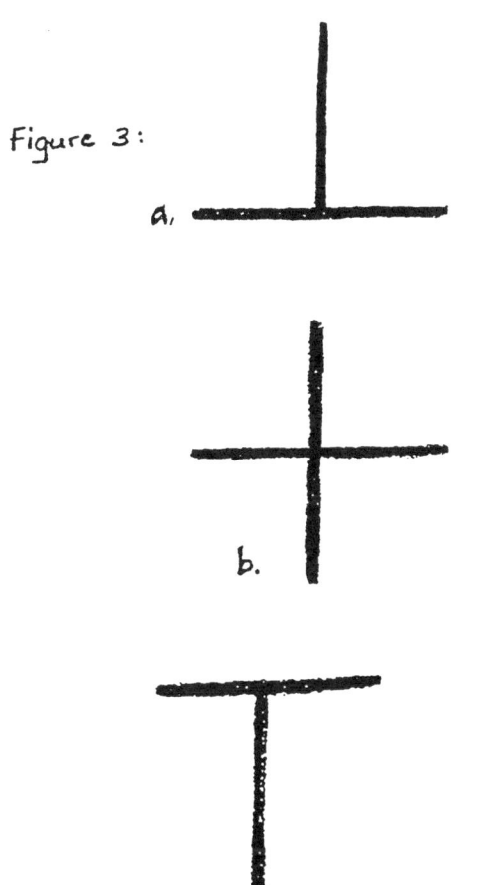

Figure 3:

a.

b.

c.

leaning lines together in a cross of Saint Andrew (Figure 5). If we teachers wish to develop a feeling for the quality of this form, we may think of the meditation we adults do in eurythmy as we think, "Weight bears downwards," for the lower limbs as we imagine the color blue and "Light streams upwards" for the arms as we imagine the color yellow, and then "I maintain the middle." There is a feeling, then, in this form, of an openness to what comes from the spiritual world as it is related to our connection with the Earth; we can feel an inner sense of balance. (Of course, we don't discuss this with the children.)

The nature of the Saint Andrew's cross is different from the nature of the cross the children have made earlier (Figure 3b). The latter also has a feeling of balance, of course, but this is the balance between freedom (the vertical line representing the Ego) and love (the horizontal line representing the surroundings).

After doing these straight line forms, it is time to begin some exercises with the curved line. The first exercise can be the circle (see Figure 6). This will not be easy for the children, so the teacher must see to it that they practice it many times before putting it on paper. It is not necessary that they *never* lift the pencil, but the line should be as continuous as possible. The next exercise with the curved line can be concentric circles, evenly spaced. The circles are drawn in the order of largest to smallest--outside in (see Figure 7). This can have the therapeutic effect of bringing the child into his body in a healthy way.

Spiral forms are next in the sequence of curved lines. Begin with very simple curves (see Figure 8).

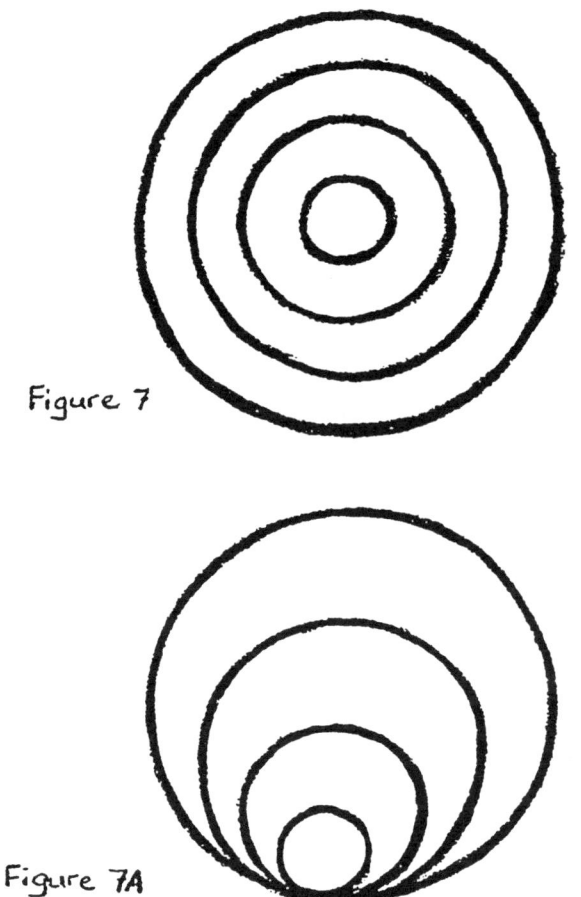

Figure 7

Figure 7A

These can be used in working with the temperaments: the melancholic or phlegmatic child should begin with Figure 8a and b, going outside in, and then she may do Figure 8c and d, going inside out. Next, the directions may be combined within the same form (see Figure 9). Different colors can be used for the different directions. A story, or picture, that the teacher might give the children for drawing Figure 9a is: A tiny little anxious boy saw a thunderstorm and was frightened, so he wanted to hide and ran indoors. He went right under his bed, which he felt must be the safest place (Come to the end of the spiral.) After a while, though, he began to feel hungry. He listened for the crash of thunder but couldn't hear it any longer (Start coming out again) so he crept out to go find his mother.

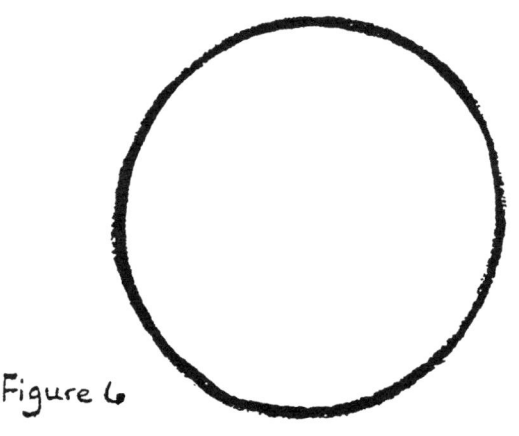

Figure 6

4

Figure 8

Figure 9

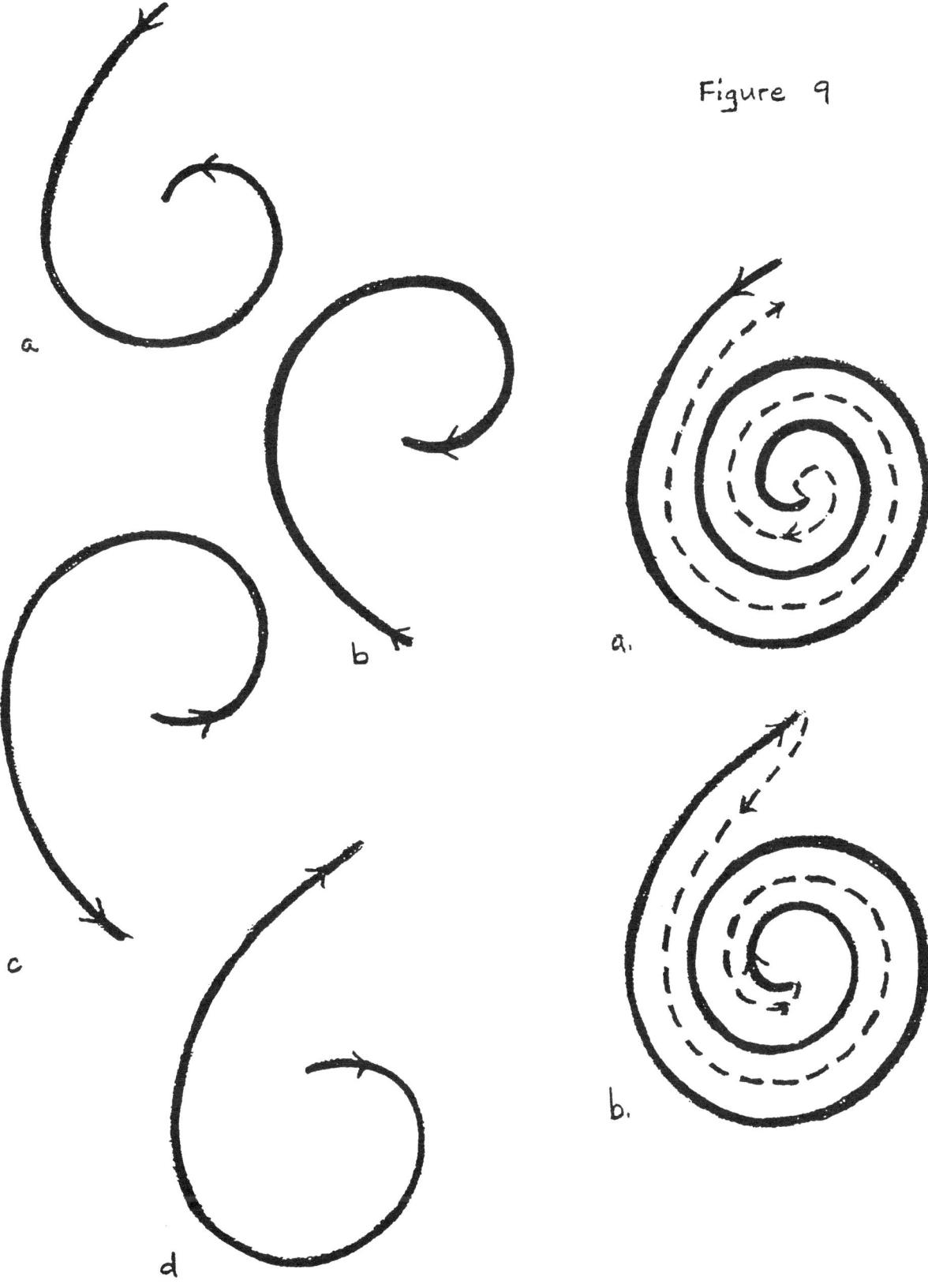

a

b

c

d

a.

b.

It is helpful to do both the spiral in the direction of the Archimedes spiral (Figure 10) and the spiral similar to the Bernoulli spiral (Figure 11) with the children. The former is drawn with the equidistant lines, giving it the quality of the addition process. The latter is also called "the spiral of logarithms" and the spaces between the lines enlarge geometrically as the spiral moves outward, giving the quality of the multiplication process. The children's attention can now be brought to the importance of the space between the lines of a form.

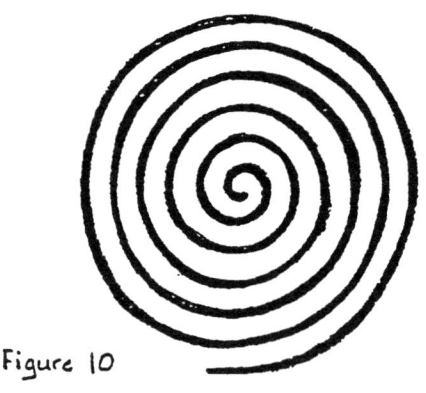

Figure 10

Another spiral with a special quality is shown in Figure 12. This form can bring the children a feeling of balance between giving and taking, between self and other. One might call it the friendship spiral. The children should have the experience of doing this spiral with their two arms, bringing their hands almost together in the middle.

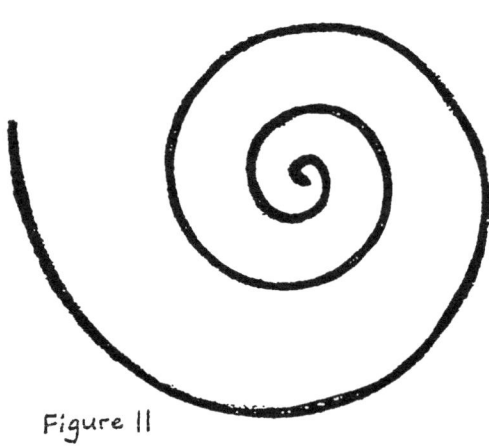

Figure 11

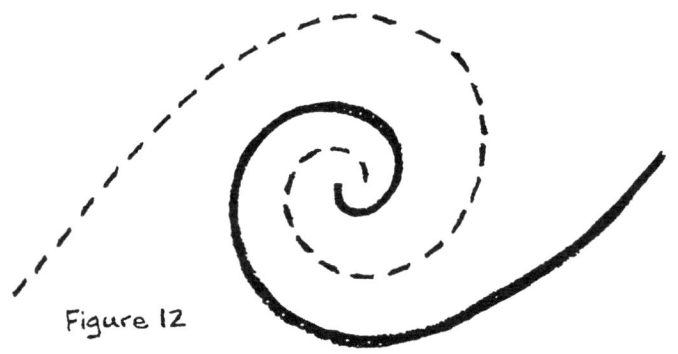

Figure 12

The form given in Figure 13 is the first curved form in which one changes directions in the middle. There are three types of singularity of line in form drawing, as shown in Figure 13. In Figure 13a, at the inflection point Z, the rotation of the line changes while the translation. or direction, of the line remains the same. In Figure 13b, at the thorn point Z', the rotation stays the same while the translation changes; the line comes back in the opposite direction. In Figure 13c, at the beak point Z", both the rotation and the translation of the line change. These three forms are really the alphabet of the curved line. As a teacher you need to be aware of how many of these points are in any form you wish to bring to your class, as they are difficult for the children. Seven of them in one form, for instance, is simply too many for a first grader.

Figure 13

A story to give the children as they practice this form is, "Here is a little girl going out for a walk (at point X); she walks a distance and you think she will come back, but (at point Z) she doesn't; she goes to visit a neighbor (end at point Y). After working this subject through, the teacher can create a few exercises for the children between Figure 13a and 14a.

Figure 14

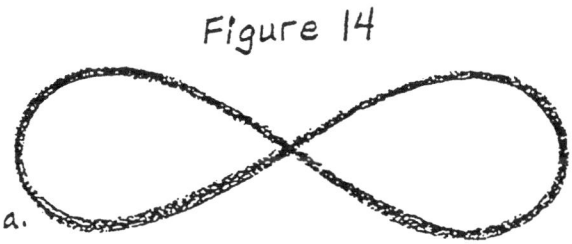

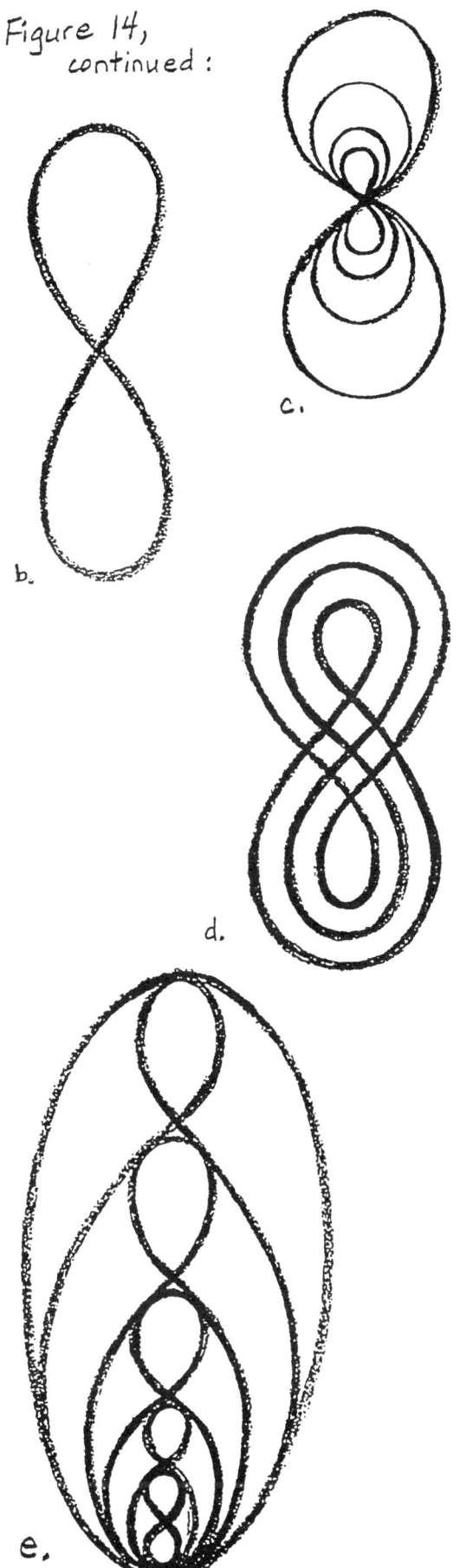

Figure 14, continued:

7

As a next step in working with the curved line and the inflection point the children may do exercises with the lemniscate (see Figure 14). They may also elaborate work with the straight line as shown in Figure 15. At this point, the teacher may ask children to see how a figure changes when its curves are changed to straight lines (see Figure 16).

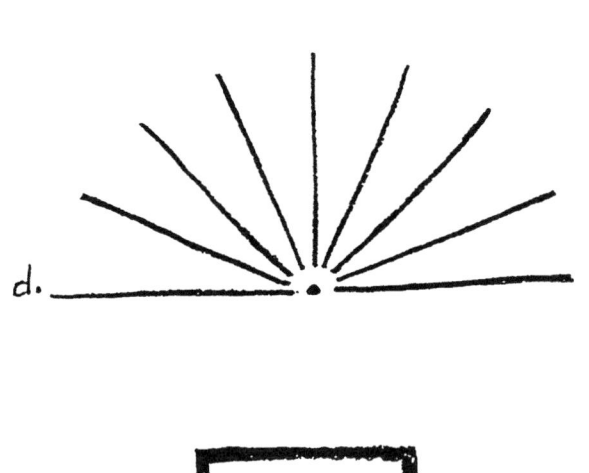
d.

Figure 15

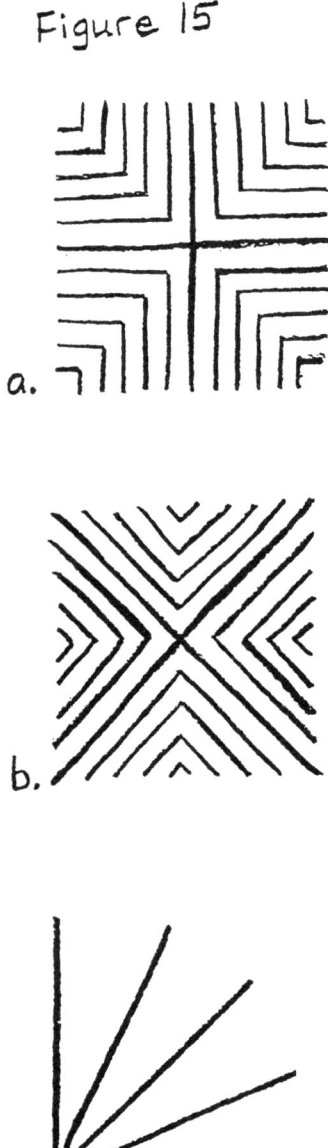
a.

b.

c.

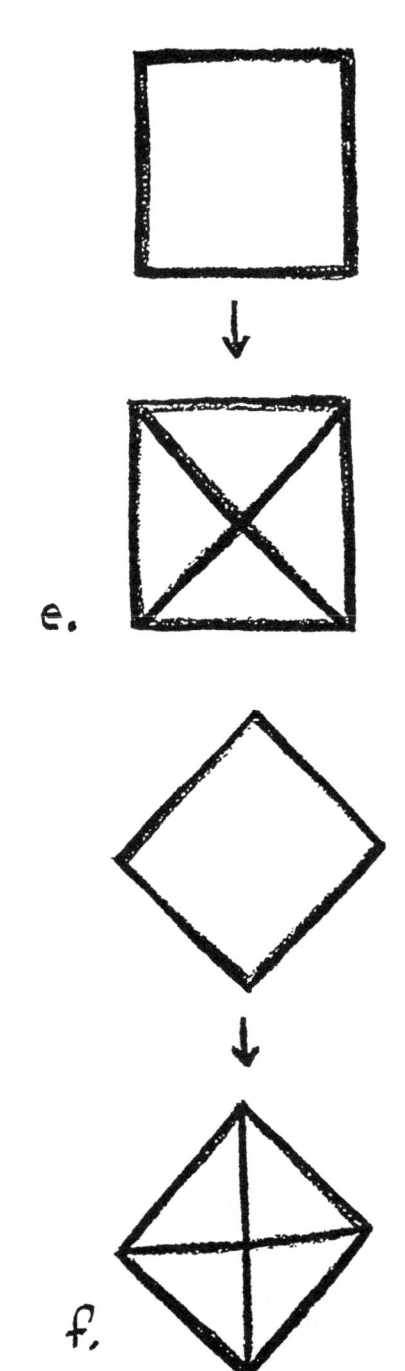
e.

f.

Figure 16

Figure 16

Figure 16 c.

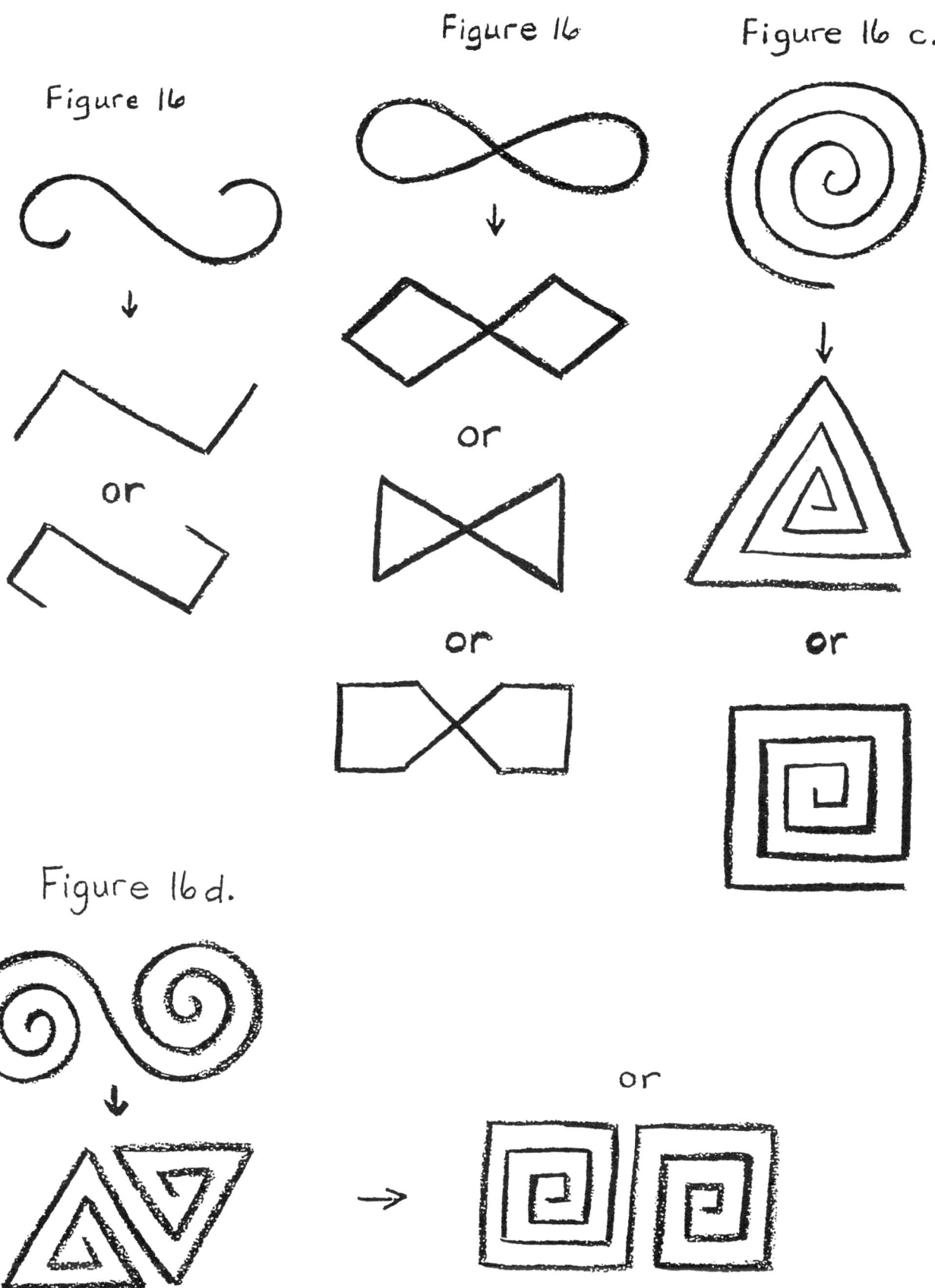

Figure 16 d.

or

Simple closed forms with a single characteristic may come next in the first grade sequence of forms (see Figure 17) The section on working with the temperaments shows some simple closed forms, but these are not part of the continuum of forms and should be done often.

children. Figure 18 is an example from Niederhauser and Frohlich. Use color to show how the inside comes to the outside and vice versa. The will activity is not actually shown in the forms themselves but in between the different forms, so it is good to ask the children what is going on between one form and

Figure 18 :

Figure 17

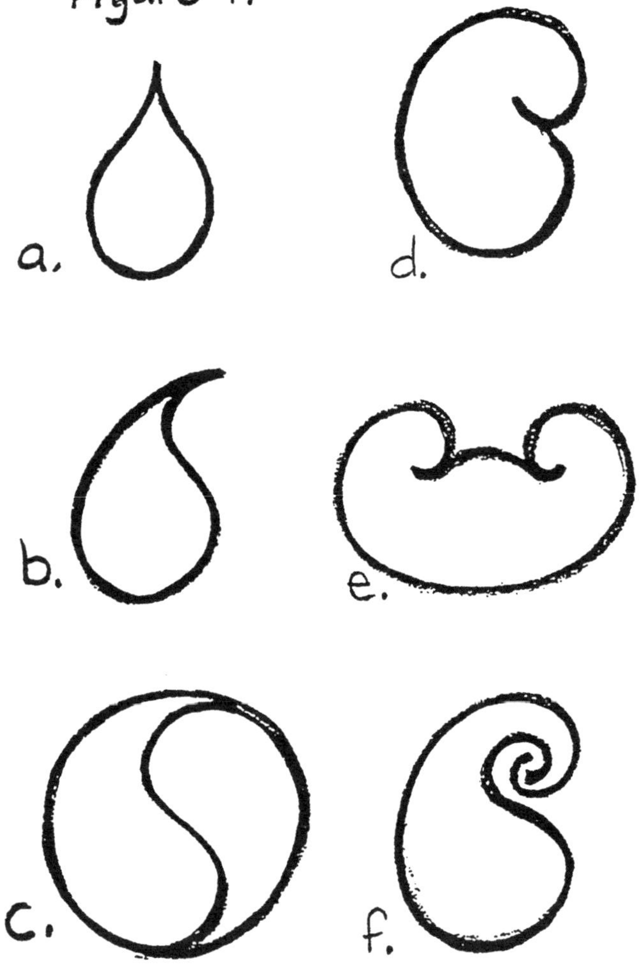

a.

b.

c.

d.

e.

f.

a.

b.

c.

d.

e.

f.

g.

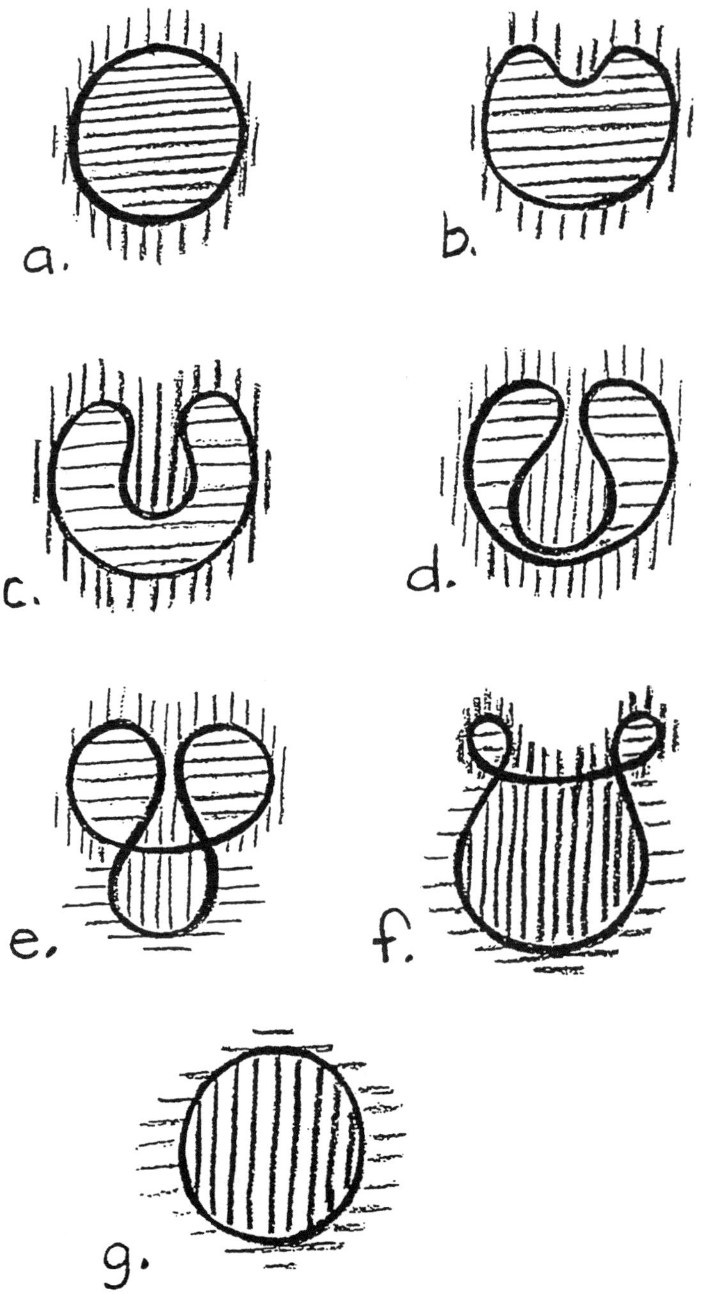

After working with the simple closed forms, the children can work with a sequence of forms showing a metamorphosis. The teacher can use a rope on the floor to go through the metamorphosis of forms with the

the next, to get them to see how (b) is formed from (a) by doing something to (a), namely pushing it in at the top.

When the children have already worked through simple closed forms and metamorphosis, they may begin working with running forms. The Kutzli wave (Figure 19) is a series of running forms which grow one out of the other. Line a is the surface of the lake on a quiet, calm day. A gentle breeze comes and the lake looks like line b. The breeze turns into a strong wind and the waves now are larger as in line c. Finally, the storm comes in full strength--line d--and it is much too dangerous to go swimming. (These types of stories give an imagination of the movement of the line and, as such, they serve to focus the attention on the form.) One could go further with the wave and create line e as a separate running form. One might then bring back the practice of changing curved lines to straight (see Figures 19 f,g,h).

Figure 19, continued:

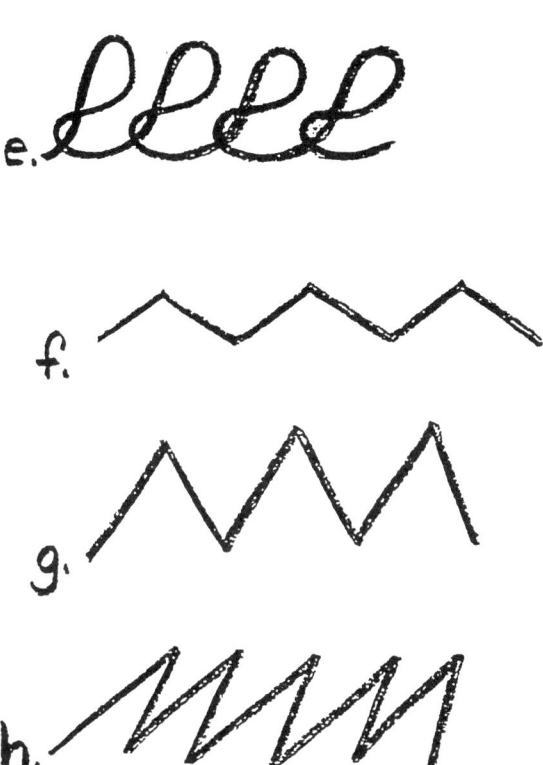

Figure 19

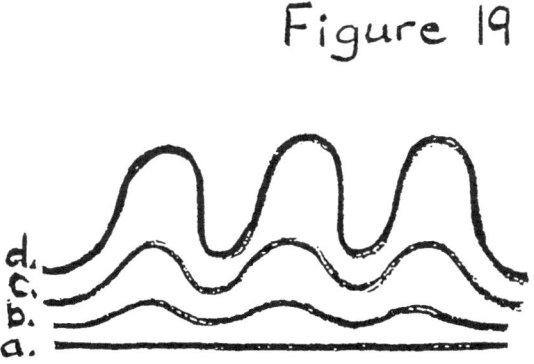

More running forms are given in Figure 20. Running forms may also be put together if they create a good balance with one another (see Figure 21). Use different colors for each form. The forms a, b, c of Figure 20 can also be used therapeutically. For a dreamy, phlegmatic child, use the sequence a, b, c. For an intellectually awake child, go the other way: c, b, a. Many other running forms are offered in Figure 20 for the teacher to select from.

11

Figure 20

a.

b.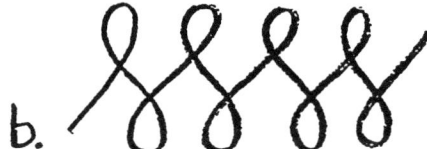

c.

d.

e.

f.

g.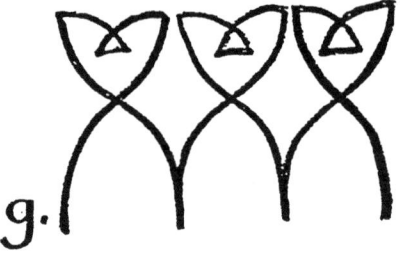

h.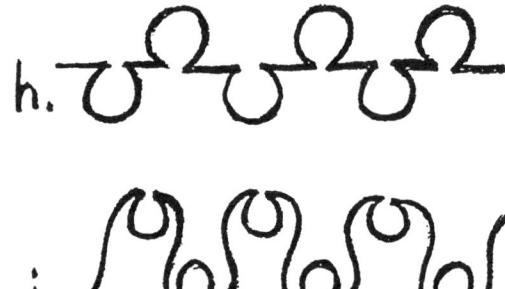

i.

j.

k.

l.

12

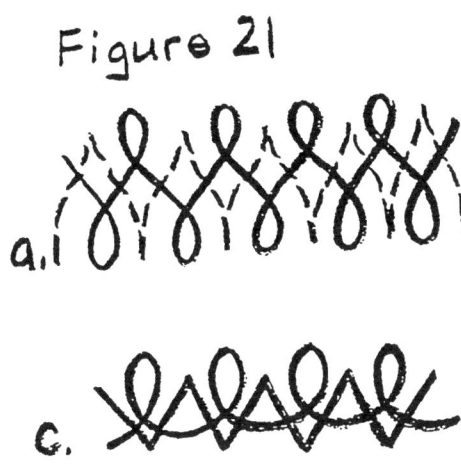

Figure 21

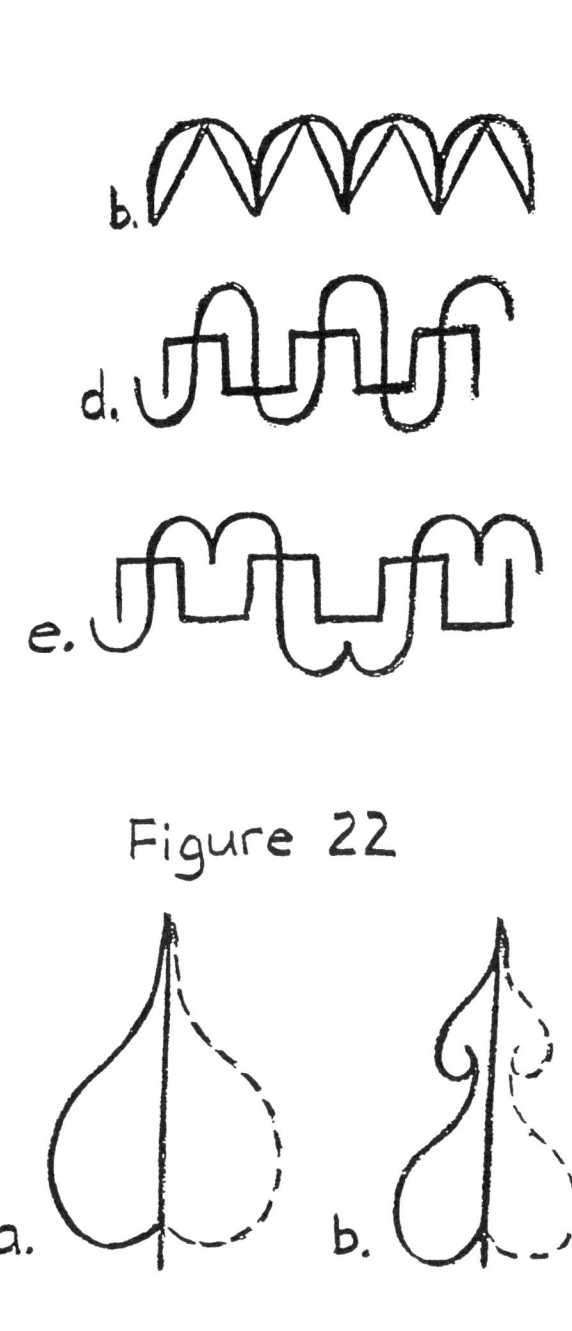

Figure 22

GRADE TWO

Mirrored, or symmetrical, forms on a vertical axis may begin near the end of the first grade or the beginning of the second grade. We take the straight vertical line from first grade and add two sides to it, making a more complicated balance. The goal is to create a harmonic balance of space. This is really the task of the second grader, who experiences a duality within of the higher and lower aspects of the self. Stories of the saints and animal fables during this year speak to the child's task. The drawing of mirrored forms also supports this.

The teacher can draw the line on the left side of the axis saying, "This is not yet complete. Who is able to finish it?" The child then finds the corresponding line on the right side (see Figure 22). For the children who draw left-handed, the teacher should draw the first line on the right. When this has been successful, the children may do the whole form themselves. Then

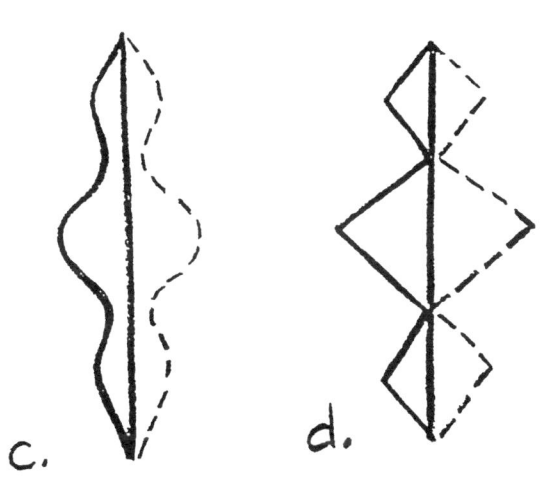

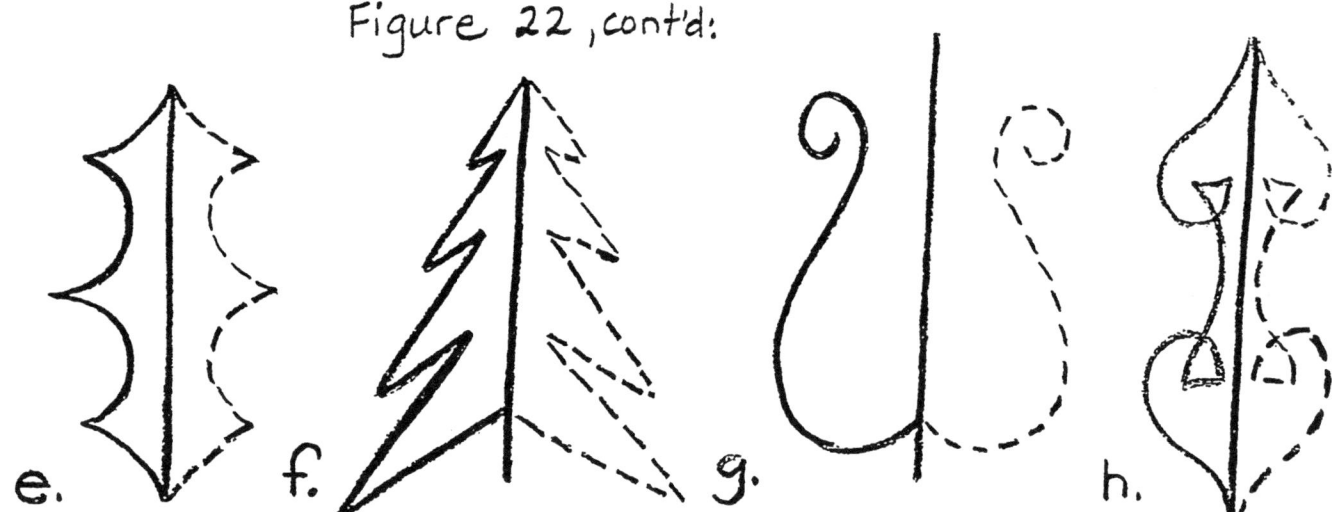

e. f. g. h.

exercises in crossing the line may be
done (see Figure 23). The horizontal
axis (the resting line from first grade)
may be used then; the teacher first
makes the line over the axis and the
child draws the corresponding line
under (see Figure 24). See Form
Drawing by Niederhauser and Frohlich
for a sequence of forms. In the late
spring of second grade, the teacher
could introduce work with both axis
lines (see Figure 25).

Figure 23

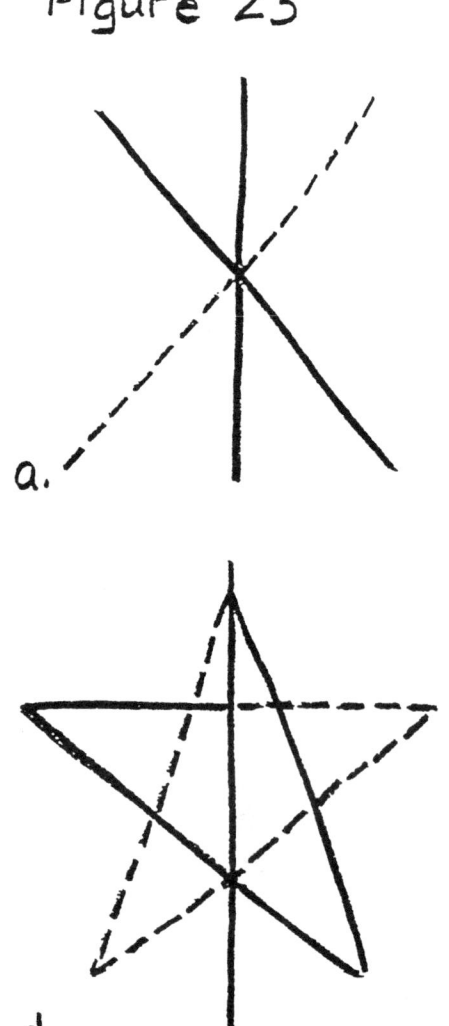

a.

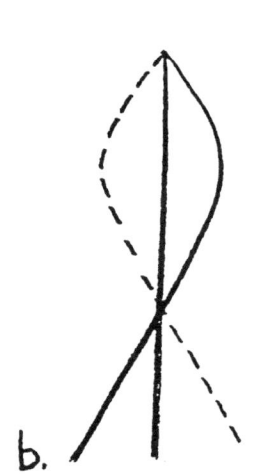

b.

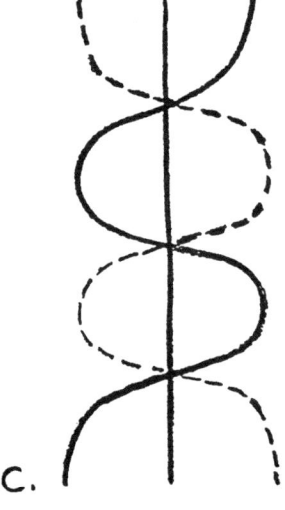

c.

d.

Figure 24

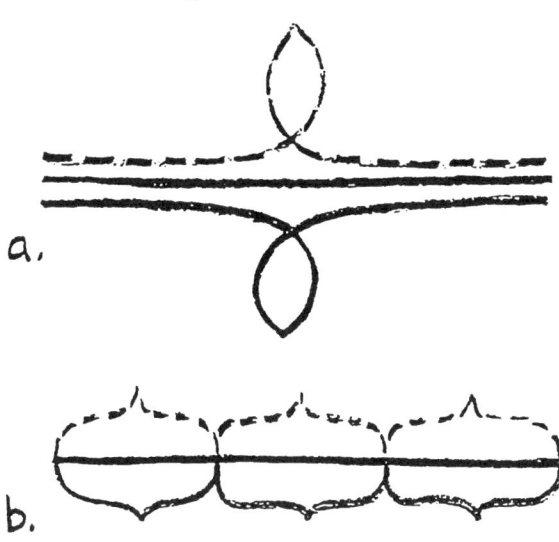

a.

b.

Figure 25

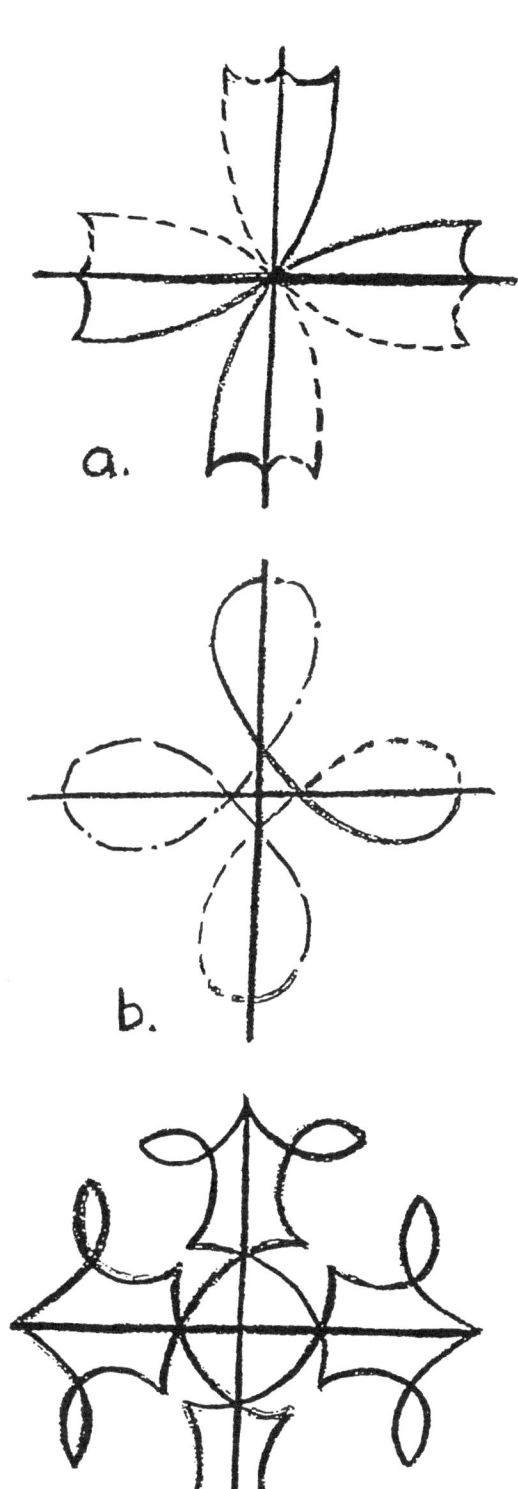

a.

b.

c.

Working with the mirrored forms can help the teacher see where a child may need special help (see Figure 26).

Figure 26

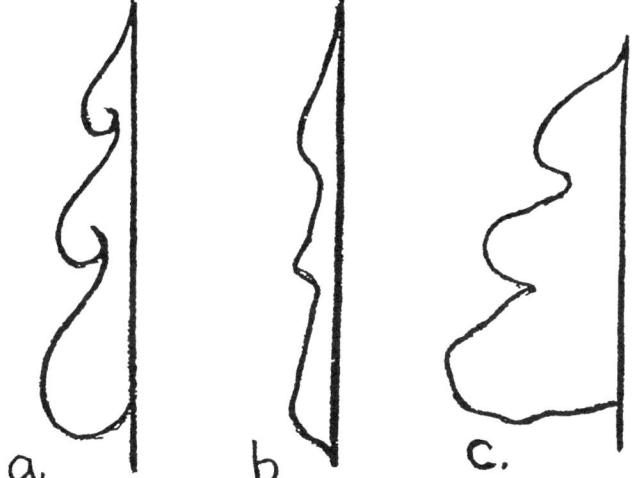

a.   b.   c.

If the teacher draws (a) and the child draws (b), this may show that the child's sense of life is weak; the life sense is deeply connected to the area of space between the lines. If the child draws (c), this can indicate that the child is not strongly enough influenced by the formative forces, that she is unsculptured, unformed. These cases can indicate that the child is not feeling the lawfulness of the forms, the balance of line and space. Space is more connected with the etheric, the line and its lawfulness with the astral. If forms like these are drawn, this could indicate that the etheric and astral bodies of the child are not in right relationship. These brief remarks are not to be taken as a sufficient base for work with handicapped children; this is only a hint. See Audrey McAllen's *Extra Lesson* for further information.

GRADE THREE

In the third grade, the year of the 9-year-change, we still work with an axis of symmetry, but the two sides are different because we use a curved axis. For the first time, the children must begin to deal with the difference between the outer and inner life. On a curved axis, one side of the form is more open to the world, one is more closed.

This is a reflection of what is happening in the child's soul life about this time. The period of the nine-year-change and how it is met by adults is critical for the child's healthy development. The child will feel an inner sense of loss, a sadness; thus, the Old Testament story of the loss of Paradise is told in the third grade. It is really a story of what the child feels inwardly to be true at this time of his life--he has lost the young child's connection to the spiritual world. The child may never express this sense of loss or sadness directly; there is now a difference between what is felt inwardly and what is spoken or enacted. In order that the child's soul life does not become split, it is essential that he or she be helped to hold the inner life and the outer life in balance. For instance, if the teacher finds out that the child has stolen something from a store or from another child and the guilty child knows that the teacher knows about it, it is good for the teacher to help the child make a balance; that is, to take the child to the store and return the stolen object. If the object was candy and has been eaten, then another way of restoring the balance must be found. The form drawing lessons for the third grade always work to aid children in finding a harmonious balance between the inside and the outside.

So the teacher brings the curved line from the first grade and draws a line on one side of it, bringing the children to see that the balancing line on the other side must be different (see Figure 27). This is related to what mathematicians call an inversion. For further explanation, see Ernst Schuberth

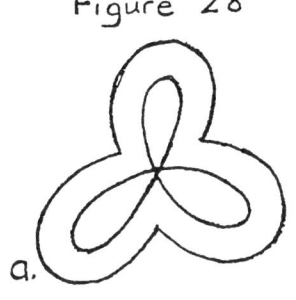

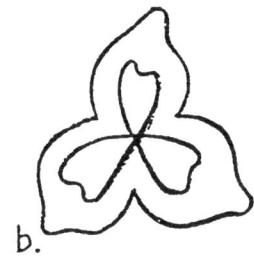

Figure 28

in Kranich, Juenemann u.a., *Formenzeichen.*

A metamorphosis of forms given by Steiner in the Ilkley course lectures illustrates how the inside line must change as the outside line changes. The teacher presents the form (Figure 28a) and the children practice it. Then the teacher changes the outer form and asks the children how the inner form could be changed to correspond. (See also Figure 29.)

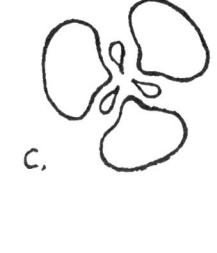

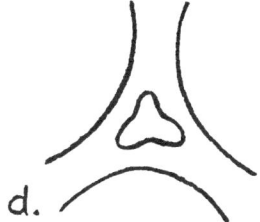

Figure 27

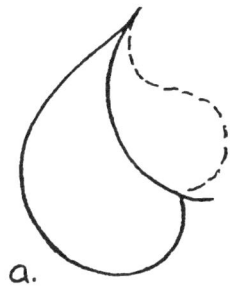

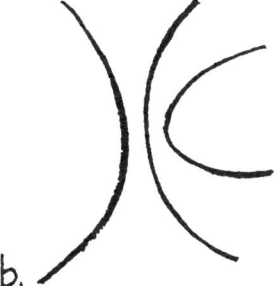

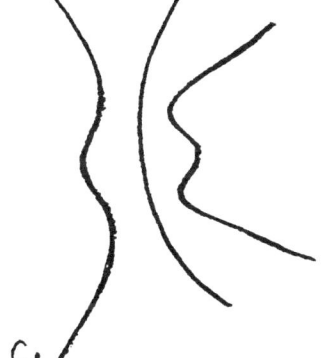

Figure 29

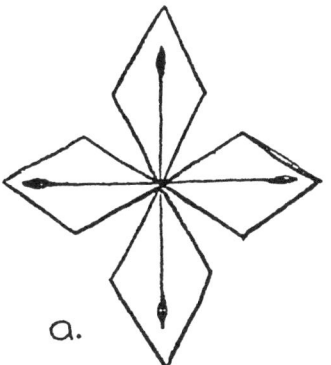

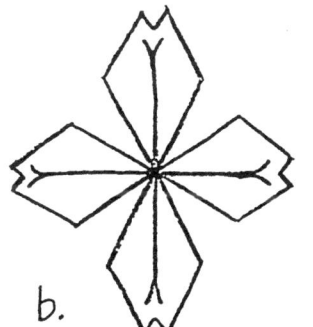

An elaboration of the third grade theme of balancing the inside and outside with one another is given in the next series of exercises in which a form is developed around a given number of points, and the class then finds the surrounding lines that create a balanced whole (see Figure 30). Figure 30a is developed from two points, Figure 30b with three, and so on. This work recapitulates in a new way the work in first grade mathematics with the quality of numbers.

These forms already have the quality of a seal in that a seal form has an inner, middle, and outer zone. The class works to balance these three zones. Some of Steiner's seals are given in the Forms for Teachers section later in this book.

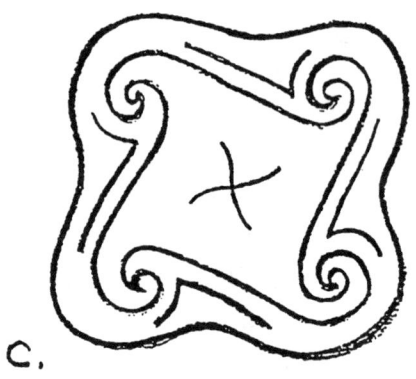

c.

Figure 30

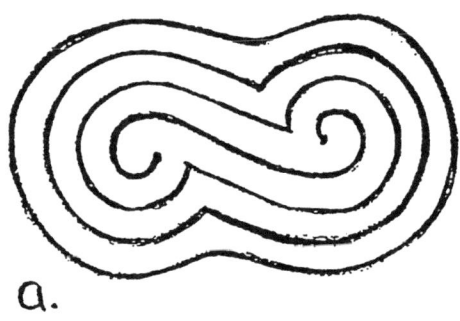

a.

d.

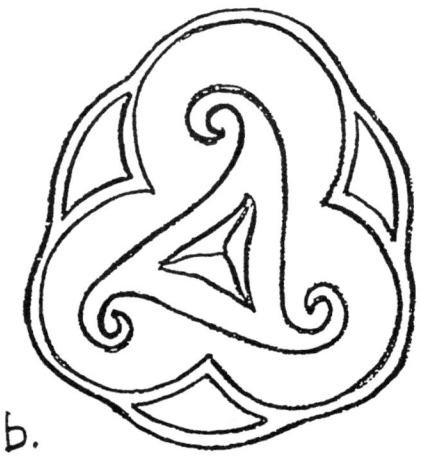

b.

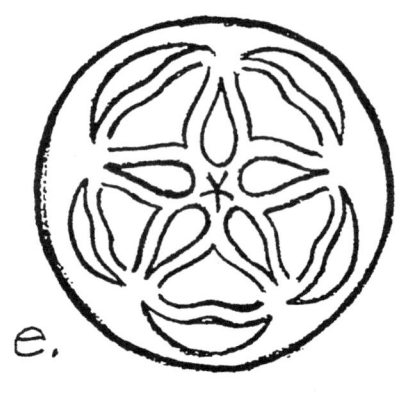

e.

Some time after the children have worked with balancing a form on a curved axis of symmetry, the idea of a free symmetry may be introduced through Steiner's form (Figure 31).

Figure 31

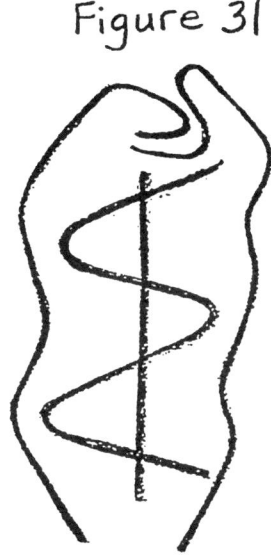

There exists in a form of this kind a dynamic symmetry, a relationship between right and left. Although the symmetric relationship is not based on geometrical laws, the form is a balanced whole.

GRADE FOUR

Fourth grade is the year the Norse mythology is brought to the children. The Norse gods are powerful, but life is a struggle for them in a way that it is not for Yahweh of the Old Testament. Yahweh is the authority and so mighty that the power of other gods becomes nothing to his. The Norse gods, on the other hand, are not so omnipotent.

The changes in Loki throughout the tales, beginning with his being humorously mischievous and ending with his having transmuted into a purely malevolent being, illustrates the gamut of evil against which the gods must struggle. Ultimately, they lose and the time of the Ragnarok (Twilight of the Gods) ensues with Baldur's death. They are left only with a glimmer of hope of renewal in the distant future, dependent on what human beings manage to accomplish.

The old clairvoyance and connection with the Gods must die so that modern consciousness can arise. The Age of Norse myths meets the fourth-graders' consciousness perfectly. They are newly awakened intellectually. They can begin to feel that life is a struggle, so they can identify with the struggles of the Gods. This struggling, fighting, brings consciousness. A true friend is someone we can fight with and not always have to be polite; a true argument allows us to form our thoughts and look at them, making adjustments and corrections as we go along, without fear, so that we can discover the truth. In Norse mythology, if a warrior died fighting without fear, he met his Valkyrie, his higher self--he met his Truth.

This awakening to Truth in a new way is what the fourth-grader is experiencing. He can follow a line of thought that weaves under and over, behind and through other thoughts. Thus the knotted forms are appropriate for this age. Working with these forms strengthens the newly-awakening force in the brain. Knotted forms are found in cultures all over the world--Japan, the Middle East, Ireland, Great Britain, Italy, Norway, etc. They are done in a very free way in Northern Europe so we use these as our main model.

Beautiful examples of these forms can be found on the stave churches in Norway. The people of this culture were a bit wild; they were fighters, like their Gods. The stave churches were decorated with intricate carvings of knotted dragons by the door, so the people were confronted on Sunday morning with the picture of their own wildness (perhaps manifested the night before in a brawl). This would act as an awakening for them to their astrality and lead them to the intention of learning to gain control over it with the Ego forces.

A picture of the struggle with the evil in ourselves and of the inner strength we need to call on to gain sovereignty over our astral forces is what we need to bring to the children at this age. The knotted forms really have a three-dimensional quality. For the child, this signifies a moving out into the physical world in a new way; it is moving into the physical world with the force of thinking in a non-intellectual way. In third grade, the children worked with the force of will into the physical world by building, cooking, etc. Fourth graders need to bring this movement to consciousness. From a deeper point of view, we can say that this is healthy for the blood, the carrier of Ego forces.

The teacher draws the form on the blackboard and the class draws it in the air, following the movement with hand and eye, saying aloud, "Behind, under, in front, over..." This gives them a feeling for the three-dimensionality of the form. The class should also use rope to make some simple knots and then draw them.

They should begin by drawing the form in the air. They may use lead pencils to get the whole form on paper; after this, they may erase and adjust and carefully draw the form. It is helpful to use shading because it accentuates the three-dimensional quality of the knotted form. To begin, take up the motif of the geometric figures from the earlier grades. Begin with the triangular knotted form, go to the square, then the pentagram, etc. (see Figure 32). Other simple knotted

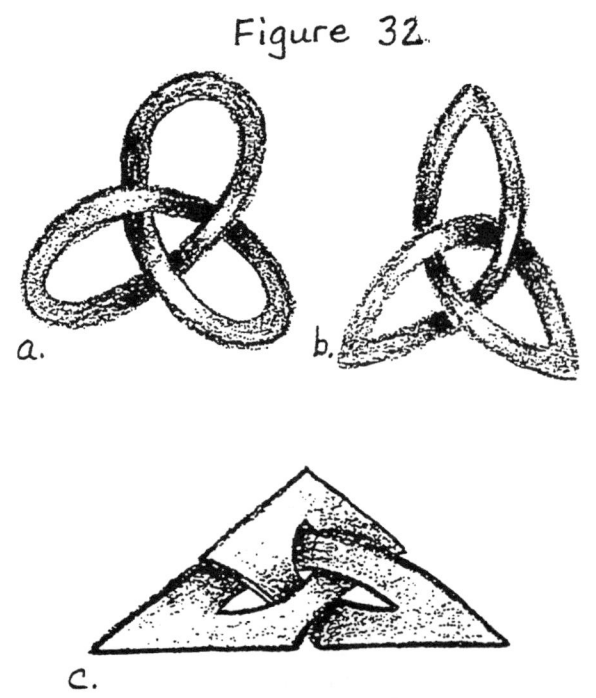

Figure 32

a.

b.

c.

20

forms are the square knot and the slip knot. (see Figure 33). A simple knot to begin with can be made with a rope around the child's arm; the arm can be the mast of a Viking ship. The child removes the rope and draws the knot form from memory. This may be done from different perspectives, so the teacher should tell the children to look at the knot from all sides while it is still on their arms (see Figure 34).

Many forms are given here for the teacher to choose from. Eventually, the children should be encouraged to develop and draw their own forms.

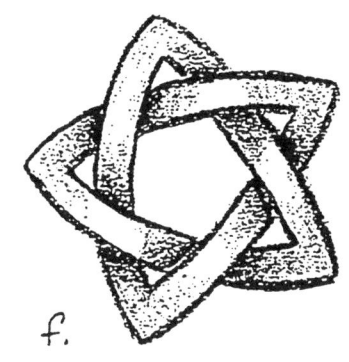

f.

Figure 33

Figure 32, continued

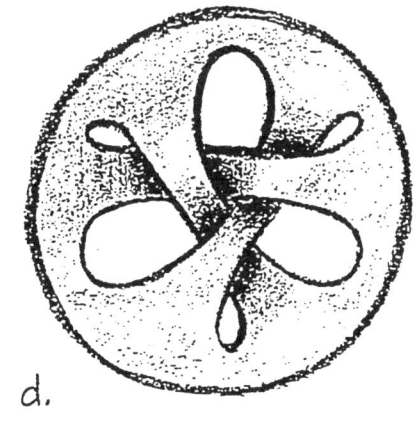

d.

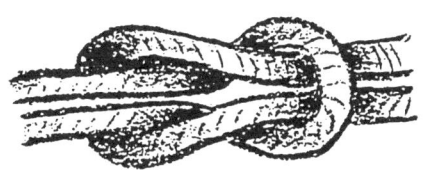

a. square knot

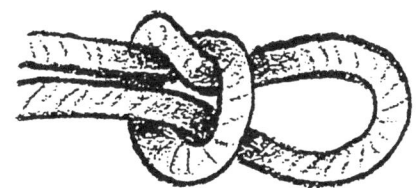

b. slip knot

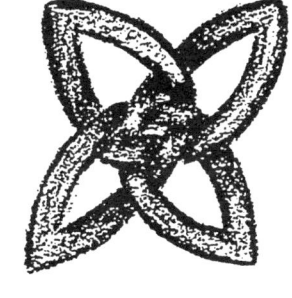

e.

Figure 34

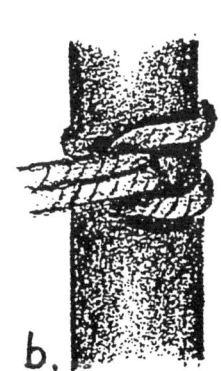

a.   b.

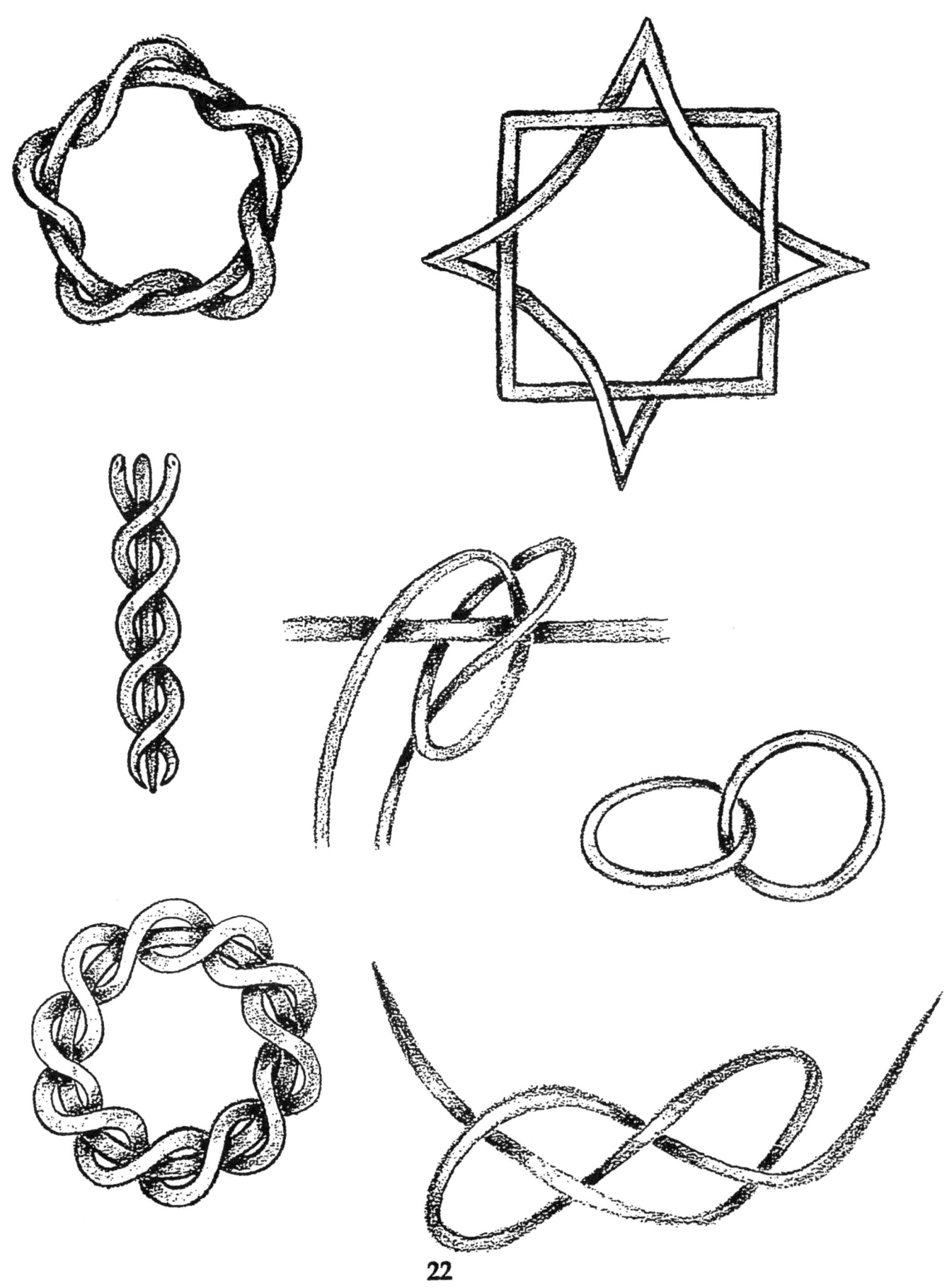

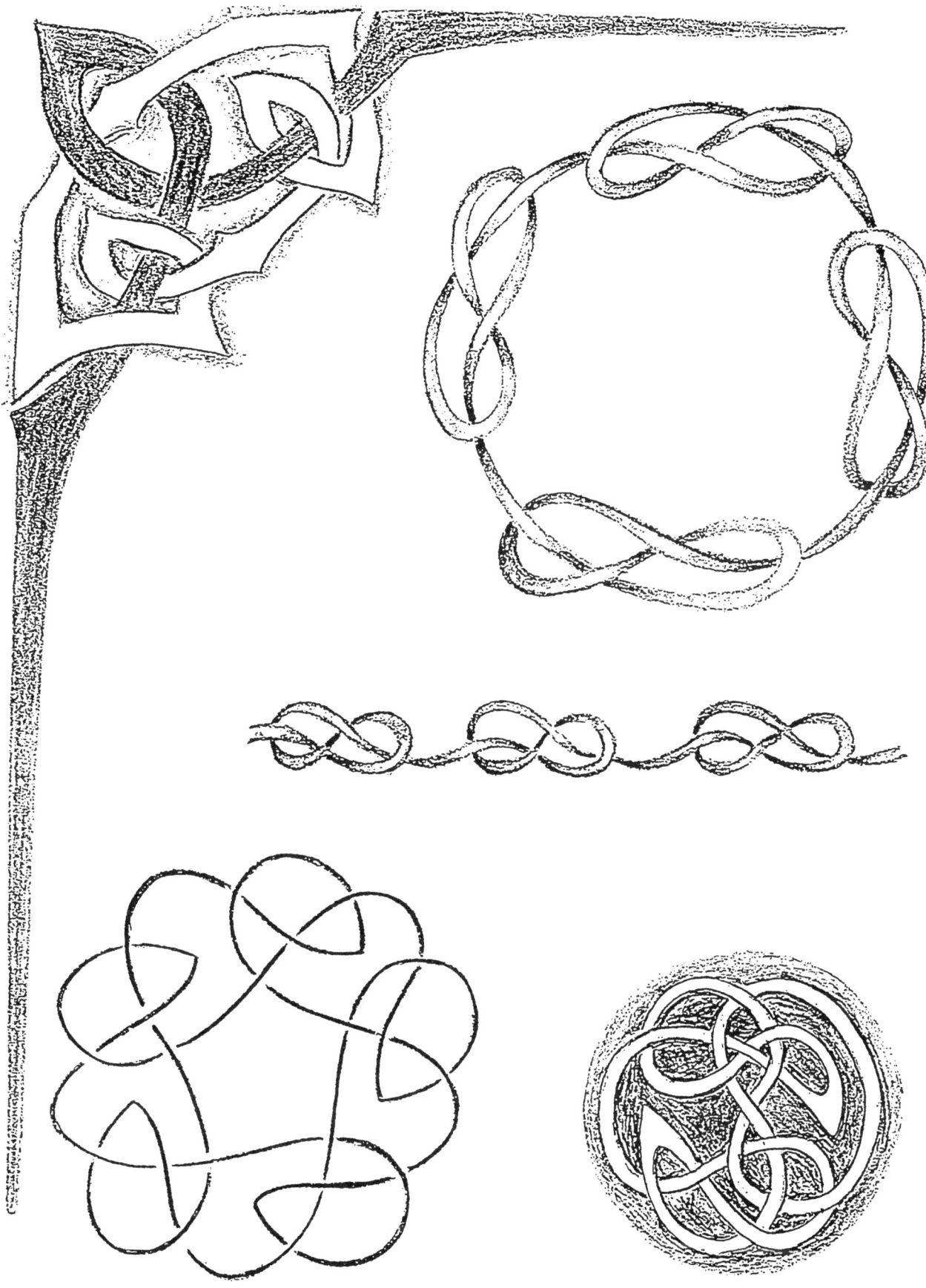

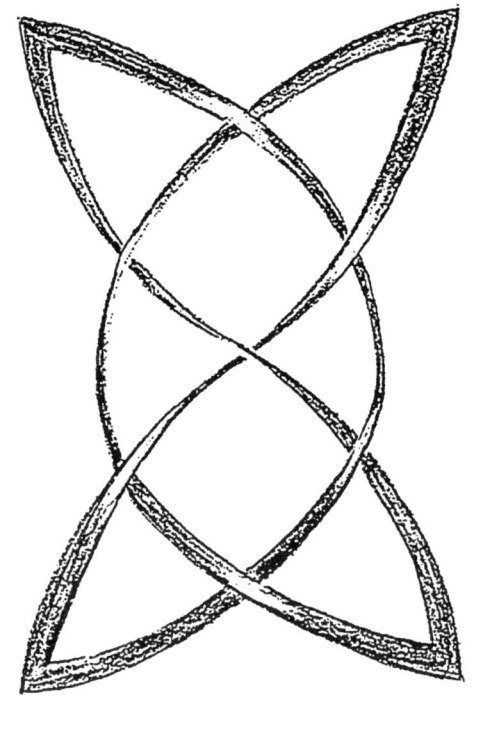

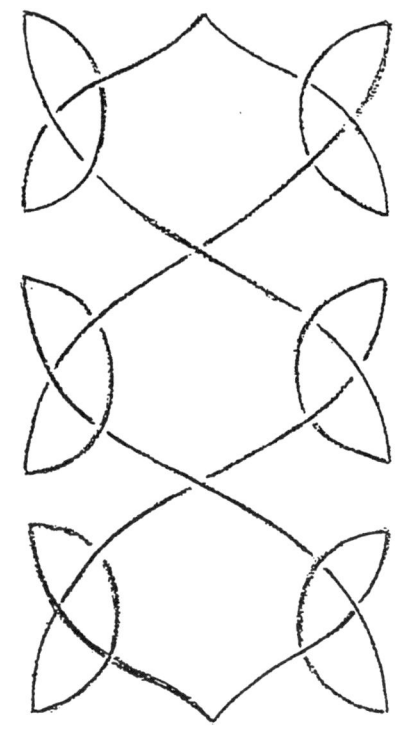

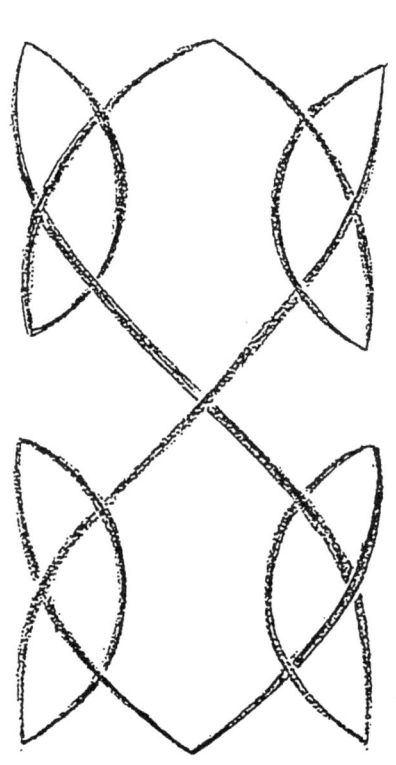

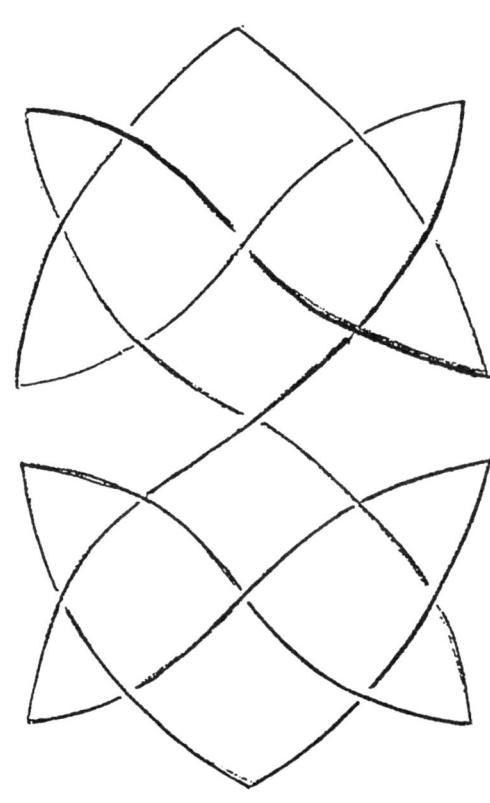

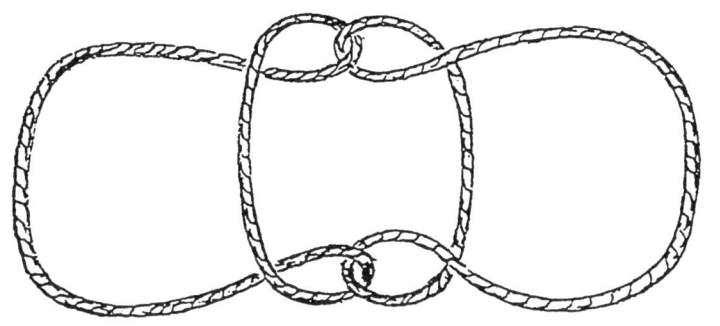

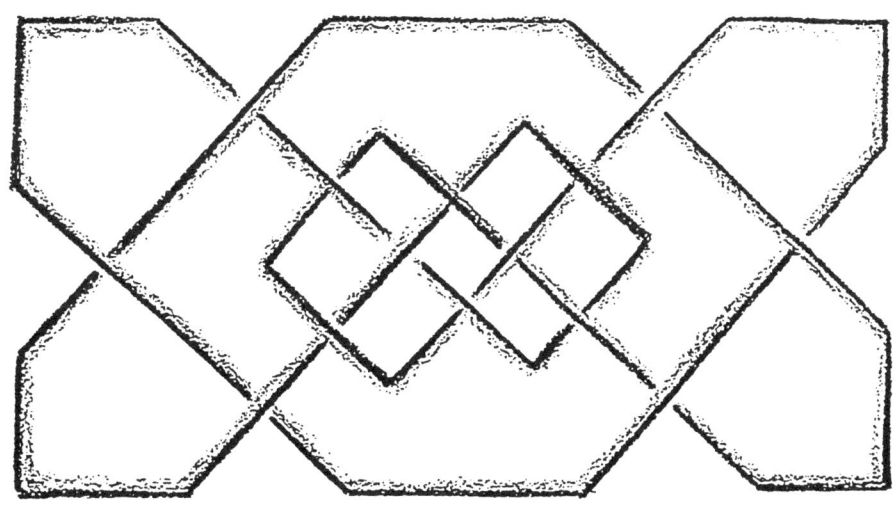

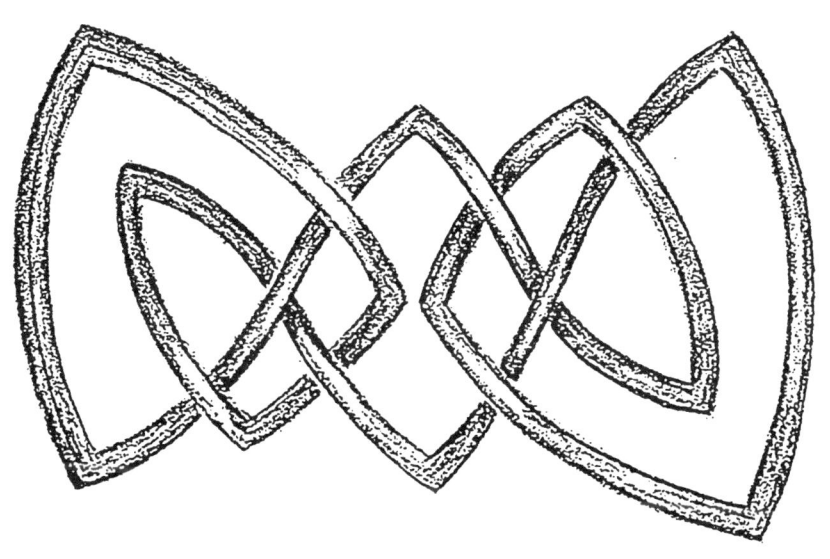

25

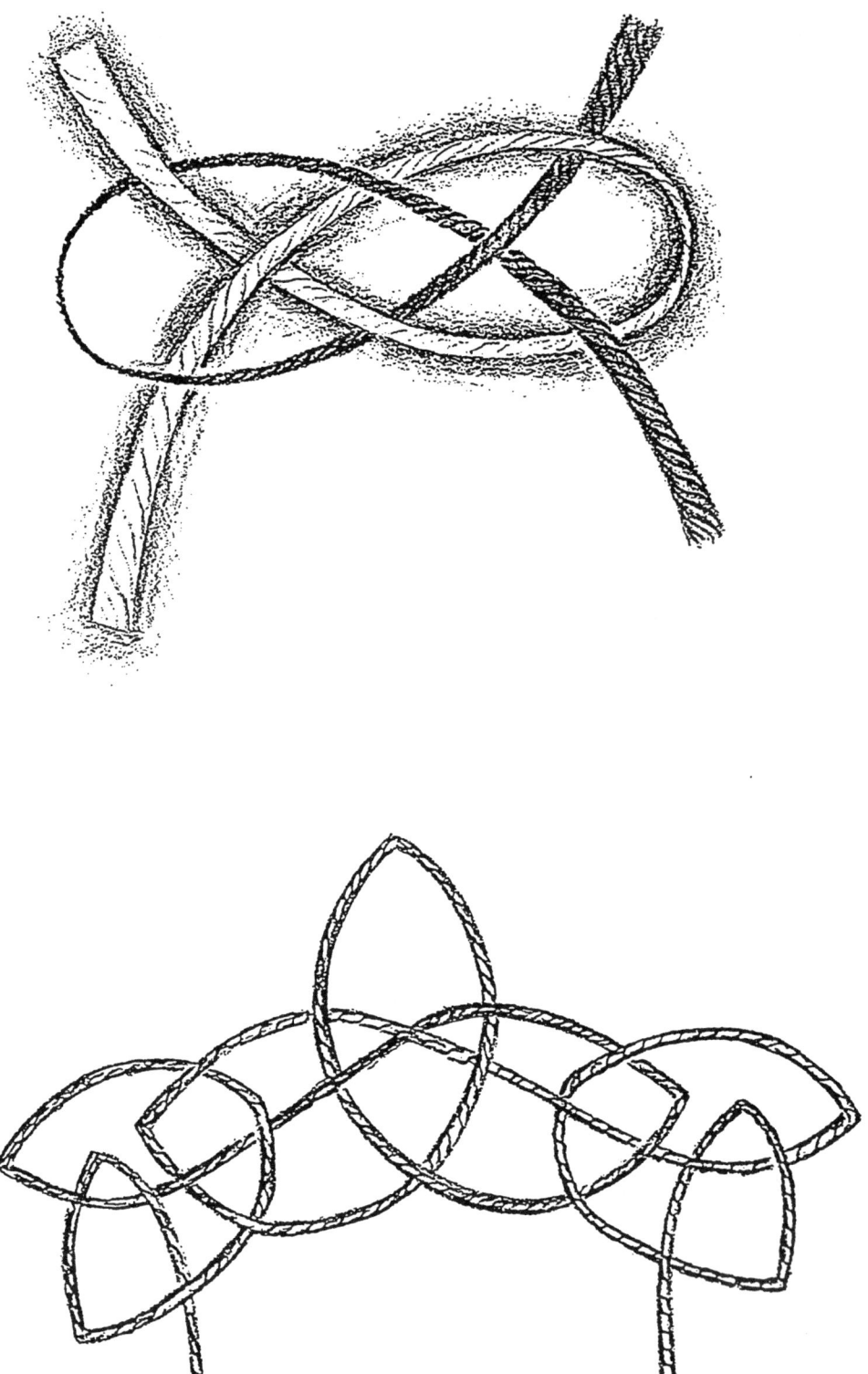

FORM AND TEMPERAMENT

Work with the temperaments must be frequent; these forms are not part of a sequence and may be done at any point in time. As always in any kind of work with the temperament, one must honor the temperament, go with it, if one is to be successful at bringing balance. See Steiner's *Discussions with Teachers.*

PHLEGMATIC

Forms for the phlegmatic temperament gently bring the child into relationship with the outer world. The phlegmatic temperament wants naturally to enclose itself; the purpose of the form drawing is always to balance the tendency of the temperament. First, then, the child draws a circle, afterwards adding the inner form (Figure 1a). When the latter is complete, the child erases the circle so that the inner form is brought into connection with the surrounding space. (Figure 1b).

CHOLERIC

Forms for the choleric temperament give the child what the phlegmatic has naturally, an enclosure for inner life. The choleric's tendency is to leap out into the world; the edges require some softening in order that the child may develop in a right way socially. The child begins by drawing the inner form, one that is choleric in nature, and then he surrounds it with a circle or softening, balancing "skin".

Phlegmatic

Figure 1

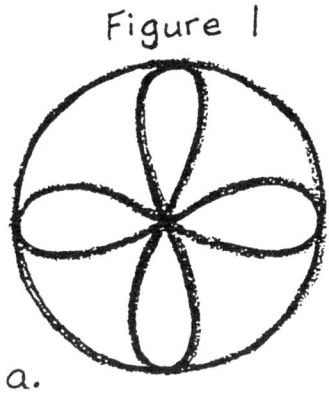

a.

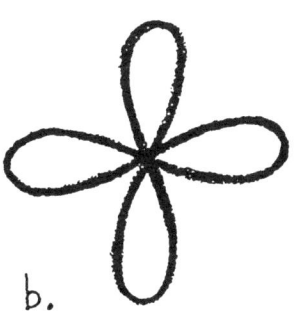

b.

Choleric

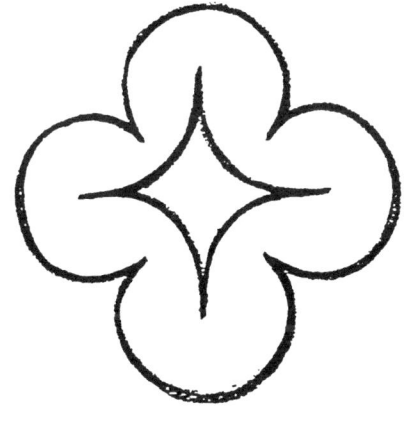

27

SANGUINE

The sanguine temperament is easily drawn out into the surroundings and needs help to return to centeredness. The forms for balancing the sanguine temperament begin by increasing, which is what the temperament naturally wants to do, and end by decreasing.

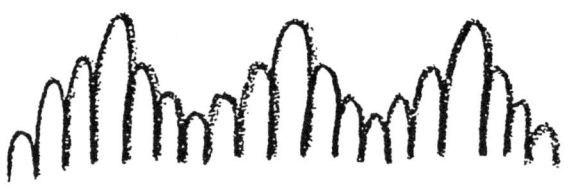

Sanguine

MELANCHOLIC

The melancholic child needs something to think about; he needs to approach a given problem thinking, "What does this mean? What does the teacher want me to do?" The forms for the melancholic must honor the deep inner life of this temperament and then bring a lightness into it. The tendency of the melancholic is to be led by the vivid inner life into dark depths. The depths must be acknowledged and light brought into them. The melancholic needs a protected place for the inner life. Thus, this temperament begins with the darkness, bringing the form to light by means of the dark. This child does the negative image of the phlegmatic's form by shading from the outside toward the inside and leaving the inner form as a space of light. This type of form requires more focussed concentration than the others, thus suiting the melancholic nicely.

Melancholic

28

FORMS FOR TEACHERS

The teacher's own inner striving and development in relationship to forms drawing (as in all aspects of life) is the single thing that will most affect the development of the children she is teaching. The forms given here, seals from Rudolf Steiner, are offered to the teachers as an opportunity to continue their development.

In the seals, all aspects of form drawing come together: the character of the lines and the space between them, metamorphosis, the relationship between the outside and the inside. The whole form really *is* something; it speaks to us. It is really the Word, the expression, of Being. Working with the seals requires much more of us than a mere intellectual understanding; it is a meditation, a part of the inner work.

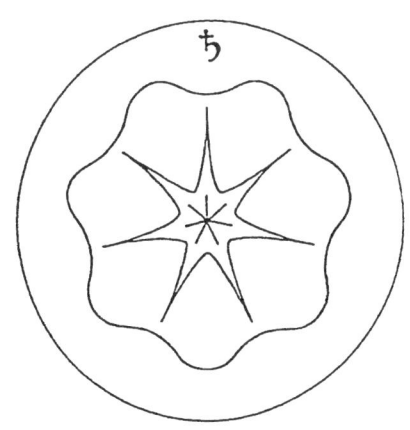

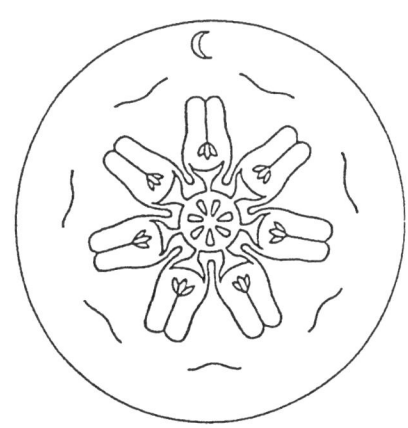

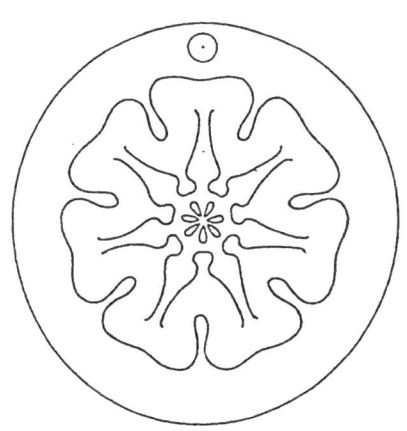

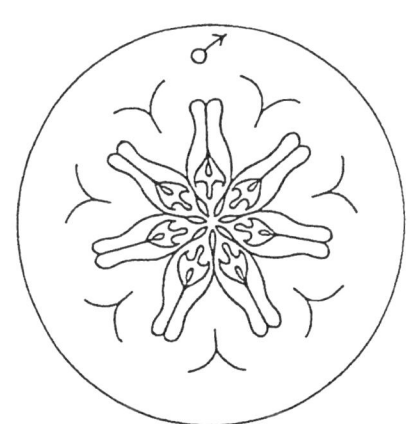

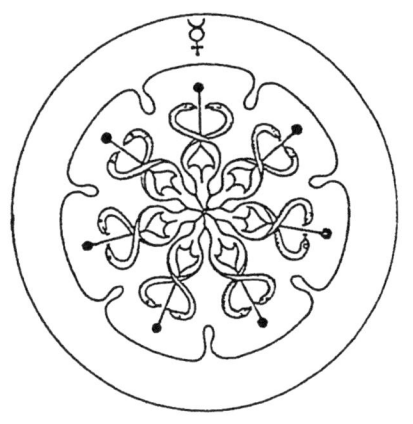 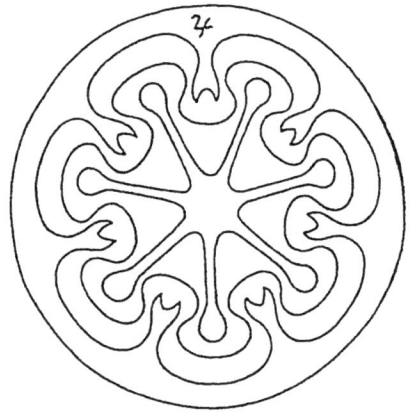 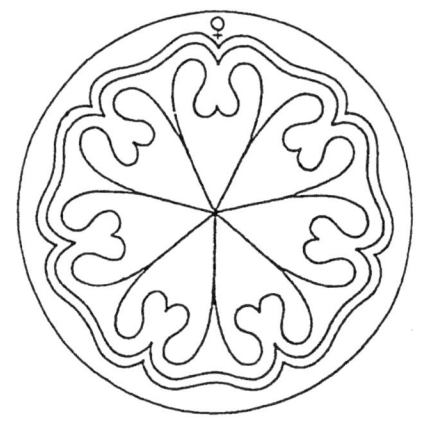

AFTERWORD

Form drawing is a path of development for the child. First, to draw meaningful forms educates the will of the child so that the will can develop into thinking. If the will is unformed and unguided in childhood, the thinking in adulthood is sloppy, scattered, and the forces of creativity cannot enliven it because no form is present to embody them. Second, form drawing has a therapeutic quality in that it develops and strengthens the constitution. Third, because form drawing develops in the human being a feeling for form and proportion, it has the capacity to imbue our culture with greater beauty. Drawing meaningful forms, then, for the first four years of grade school, is an activity that carries great significance for the human being.

In the fifth grade, form drawing changes into geometric drawing. Nevertheless, some teachers again and again come back to form drawing connected to history and the different cultures taught in the curriculum by, for instance, taking a marvelous example from a particular culture and working with it to put it in a main lesson book.

In the seventh grade, many children have a tendency to make forms which are inessential or fantastic; we, as teachers, have to notice whether the forms actually say something or are spiritually empty. If we integrate form drawing into the curriculum, we continue to guide the children in making well-proportioned, artistically rich forms. If we do this through the eight grades of the lower school, the children can develop a strong feeling for the lawfulness of forms, which will enable them to feel the lawfulness of mathematical functions in high school.

30

BIBLIOGRAPHY

Bain, George
The Methods of Construction of Celtic Art, Glasgow

Brater, Michael/ Elsasser, Peter/ Zastrow, Wilfried J.
Dynamisches Formenzeichnen, Gesellschaft fur
Ausbildungsforschung und Berufsentwicklung e. V., Bd. 1, Munchen und
Mering 1993

Clausen, Anke-Usche und Riedel, Martin
Zeichnen = Sehen lernen, Stuggart 1968

Davis, Courtney
Celtic Art Source Book, London 1988
Celtic Iron-On Transfer Patterns, New York 1989

Kranich, Ernst-Michael/ Junemann, Margrit/ Berthold-Andrae, Hildegart/ Buhler, Ernst/ Schuberth, Ernst
Formenzeichnen, Die Entwicklung des Formensinns in der Erziehung,
Stuttgart 1992

Kutzli, Rudolf
Entfaltung schopferischer Krafte durch lebediges Formenzeichnen.
Ein Ubungsweg in 12 Folgen, Folgen 1 - 6, Schaffhausen 1987
Entfaltung schopferischer Krafte durch lebendiges Formenzeichnen
Ubungsweg in 12 Folgen, Folgen 7 - 12, Schaffhausen 1987
Enfaltung schopferischer Krafte durch lebendiges Formenzeichnen,
Erganzungsheft, Schaffhausen 1987

Merne, John G.
A Handbook of Celtic Ornament, Dublin and Cork 1984

Niederhauser, Hans/ Frohlich, Margaret
Form Drawing, Spring Valley, New York 1984

Petrie, Flinders
Decorative Symbols and Motifs for Artists and Craftspeople, New
York 1986

Wilson, Eva
Early Medieval Designs from Britain for Artists and Craftspeople, New York
1987